MARVELOUS Martin
An Activity Book

ISBN 978-0-692-19228-3

©Prideful Kids 2018

Written by
Dr. Candice Dawson

Art by
Shiela Alejandro

This activity workbook is dedicated to the Original Prideful Kids, Caylee and Donovan, and all Prideful Kids everywhere. May you see yourself here, everywhere you go, and in everything that you learn.
You are a GENIUS!

-Dr. D

Instill self-pride while teaching core curriculum.
Read the directions with your child and help guide
him or her through the activity workbook.
Use Marvelous Martin's Words in the back of the workbook
to help along the way.

I am Marvelous Martin! When I was born,
my name was Michael Luther King, Jr., but when I got
older I changed my name to Martin. I am a Pastor.
I believed in Christianity, love, and the ways of
Gandhi. These things lead me to be the leader I was.

I am known as the face of the Civil Rights Movement. The Civil Rights Movement
was about Blacks and Whites being treated equal and I believed in just that.
I am famous for my involvement with the Montgomery Bus Boycott ,
the March on Washington where I gave the "I Have A Dream" speech, and
"Letters from a Birmingham Jail". I was involved with the National Association
for the Advancement of Colored People (NAACP)
and Southern Christian Leadership Conference (SCLC).

On April 4, 1968, I was on the balcony of my motel room in Memphis, Tennessee
when someone decided to hurt me for what I believed.
I was only 39 years old when I died. My wife, Coretta Scott King, continued
to stand for Civil Rights after I was gone.

Language Arts

Trace and Write

Trace the capital M and lowercase m and write some of your own.
Read and trace the sentence then write your own.

M

m

Read and trace the sentence.

Marvelous Martin made miraculous moves marching miles.

Syllables

Clap your hands as you say each word out loud to find the number of syllables. Write your answer in the boxes.

Leader ☐

Dream ☐

Martin ☐

Birmingham ☐

Word Matching

Draw lines to match the word to the picture.

Pastor •

March •

Ghandi •

Letters •

Montgomery •

Rhyming

Circle the pictures that rhyme.

Which rhymes with mat?

Which rhymes with mop?

Which rhymes with mitten?

Which rhymes with mug?

Counting Page

Circle the 6 images that are the same.

Calendar

Use the calendar to find the month, day, and year Marvelous Martin was born.

January 1929

Sun	Mon	Tue	Wed	Thu	Fri	Sat
		1	2	3	4	5
6	7	8	9	10	11	12
13	14	15	16	17	18	19
20	21	22	23	24	25	26
27	28	29	30	31		

Addition

Write the number of each under each picture and add them together.
Write your answer.

Subtraction

Read each word problem and write the answer.

There were 6 [sign] 3 [sign] leave

How many [sign] are left?

Answer: ☐

Subtraction

Read each word problem and write the answer.

There were 10 at the March on Edmund Pettus Bridge.

2 leave

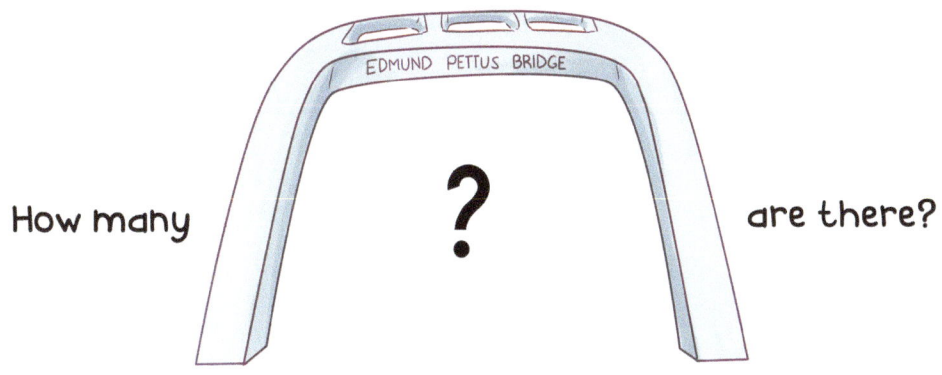

How many ? are there?

Shapes

Find the hidden 2 D shapes in the picture from the March on Washington. Square, Circle, Hexagon, Oval, Parallelogram.

Science

The Letter from Birmingham Jail

When Marvelous Martin wrote the Letter from Birmingham Jail he had to write on anything he could find.

He wrote on newspaper, sheets of paper that were secretly given to him, and even toilet tissue.
Write a secret message of your own using hidden ink.

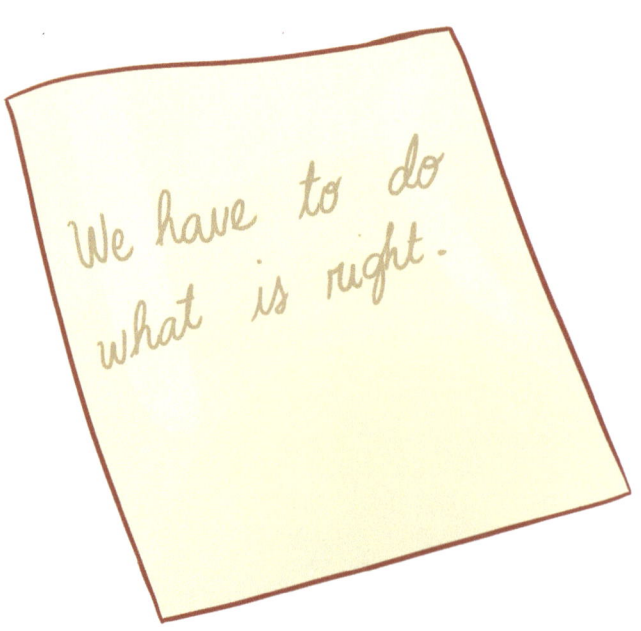

What You Need:

Lemon
(cut in half)

Bowl

Cotton Balls

Water

Spoon

White paper

Light bulb

Directions

Squeeze lemon juice into the bowl.

Add drops of water.

Stir the water and lemon juice with the spoon.

Dip the cotton ball into the water and lemon juice mixture and write a message on the white paper.

Wait for the juice to dry. Read your secret message by holding the white piece of paper to close to a light bulb.

Civil Rights and Integration

Oil, water, and dish liquid demonstrate how segregation and integration came about. Oil and water do not mix, but when you add dish liquid it allows them to come together.
The oil stands for White people in America.
The water stands for Black people in America.
The dish liquid stands for the Civil Rights Movement.

What You Need:

Water

Cooking oil (2 tablespoons)

Dish liquid

Clear water bottle or 2-liter bottle

Food coloring

Directions:

Part One:

Add food coloring to the water.

18

Pour 2 tablespoons of the colored water and 2 tablespoons of cooking oil into the water bottle or 2-liter bottle.

Screw the top on tight.

Shake the bottle as hard as you can.

Put the bottle down and let the liquids settle. You will see the liquids separate.

Part Two:

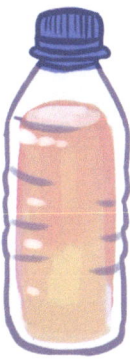

Now add some dish liquid to the mixture inside the bottle. Watch how they are joined together.

I Dream About...

Write your dreams in the clouds.

Color it!

Marvelous Martin's peaceful protests played an important role in passing the Voting Rights Act of 1965.

Maze

Help Marvelous Martin and Coretta Scott King travel over the Edmund Pettus Bridge.

Secret Word Puzzle

Each letter of the alphabet is represented by a number. Use the key to figure out the quote from Marvelous Martin's Letter from Birmingham Jail.

A	B	C	D	E	F	G	H	I	J	K	L	M
1	2	3	4	5	6	7	8	9	10	11	12	13

N	O	P	Q	R	S	T	U	V	W	X	Y	Z
14	15	16	17	18	19	20	21	22	23	24	25	26

"20 8 5   7 15 1 12   15 6   1 13 5 18 9 3 1
__ __ __   __ __ __ __ __ __   __ __ __ __ __ __ __

9 19   6 18 5 5 4 15 13"
__ __   __ __ __ __ __ __ __

Differences Appear

Circle the 5 differences in the pictures.

Marvelous Martin is awarded the Nobel Peace Prize in 1964

Crossword Puzzle

```
M T F L N J A E M A R C H P J N G T X
A C C A P H N O Y A C Q Z Y S N G O S
R X V I R Y X E V Q U G E R I E Z B
T C C Q V Y K X W Y J H A K B Q T L V
I U F N A I R M F O X O T U L O Y H A
N Z X P R L L J B G X T S P V J K A U
L Q G P C O M R N G O T R P C I E Y B
U K Y A M Z H K I C H P D L U W Q J O
T Q A H Q R G Q S G J C Q V L Z Z R H
H F C M I X I A I D H L O T I V E J C
E X J M O A T R Q S A T C B I C B A O
R T J G F T G E D A I S R F H P K T
K R C C E N J G Q O J M S L D B M N T
I I L R I F M C G U M V Y B O A M P J
N Z O T L N Y H Q X N T O U
G C O Y T X R A W Z L B J K C E F A
J V K X C A Q J T R Y E B S U Z Q G O
R B H G Q W M L V C A D O V X F M N Q N
R S E C C M F C I J Y T Q H A K R I J
```

- Boycott
- Civil Rights
- Coretta Scott King
- Equal
- March
- Martin Luther King Jr
- Voting Rights

Something is Different

Find the object that doesn't belong.

Marvelous Martin had 4 children. Their names were Dexter, Yolanda, Bernice, and Martin.

Answer Key

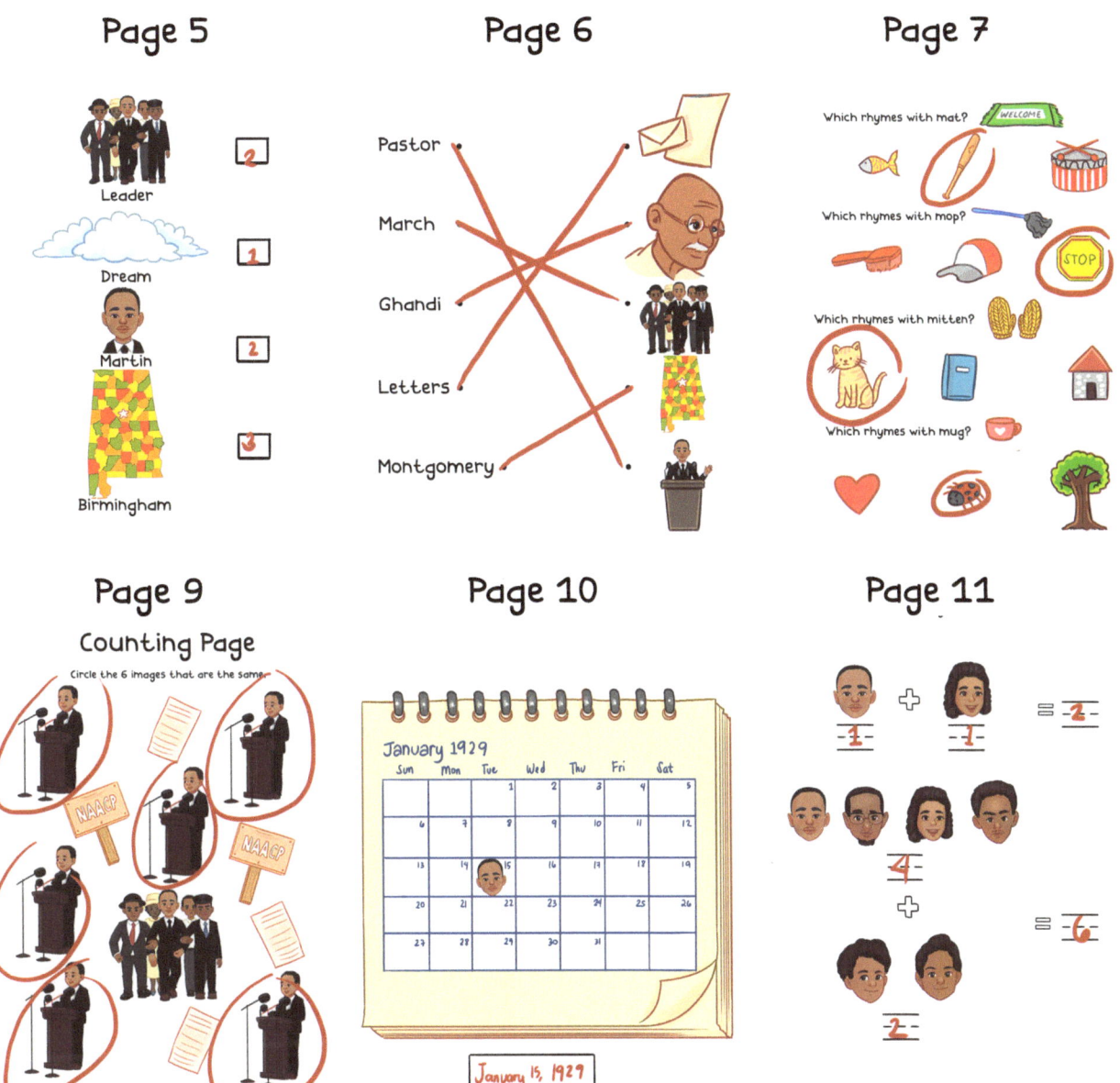

Answer Key

Page 12
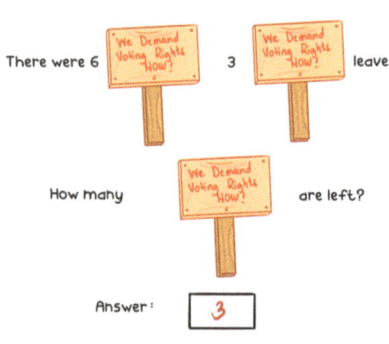

Page 13

Page 14

Page 14

Page 25
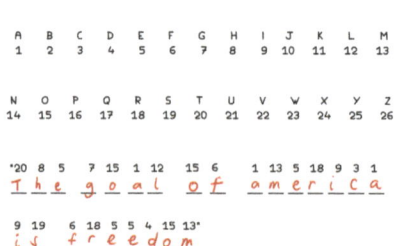

A	B	C	D	E	F	G	H	I	J	K	L	M
1	2	3	4	5	6	7	8	9	10	11	12	13

N	O	P	Q	R	S	T	U	V	W	X	Y	Z
14	15	16	17	18	19	20	21	22	23	24	25	26

20 8 5   7 15 1 12   15 6   1 13 5 18 9 3 1
The goal of america

9 19   6 18 5 5 4 15 13*
is freedom

Page 26

Page 27
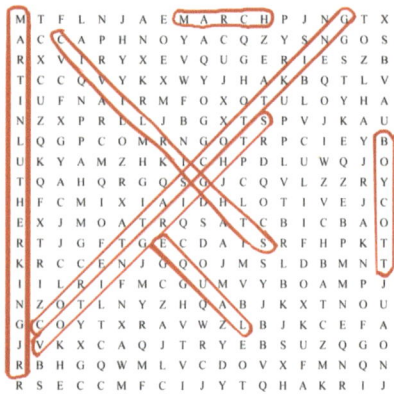

- Boycott
- Civil Rights
- Coretta Scott King
- Equal
- March
- Martin Luther King Jr
- Voting Rights

Page 28

Marvelous Martin's Words

Pastor-Person in charge of a Church.

Mahatma Gandhi-Gandhi-Political and spiritual leader that believed in non-violent ways of protest.

Leader-Person who commands a group & makes good choices even when others make wrong ones.

Civil Rights Movement-Large movement with many events against segregation. It took place from 1954-1968.

Montgomery Bus Boycott-Event in the Civil Rights Movement when African Americans in Montgomery, Alabama decided to no longer ride the bus. They did not ride the bus because they didn't like how they were treated because of their race.

March on Washington for Jobs and Freedom-March that took place in August 1963 to show how African Americans were not being treated equal and were unable to get jobs or equal pay.

I Have A Dream-A speech given by Martin Luther King, Jr (MLK). at the March on Washington. This was from a speech he had given two months earlier in Detroit, Michigan. Mahalia Jackson, a singer and activist, asked MLK to say this speech while he was reading the one he prepared during the March on Washington.

Marvelous Martin's Words

Letters from a Birmingham Jail-Jail-A letter written by MLK on April 16, 1963 while he was in jail in Birmingham, Alabama. The letters talked about non-violence being a good way to fight against racism.

NAACP-National Association for the Advancement of Colored People was started February 12, 1909 and is the oldest and largest Civil Rights organization.

SCLC-Southern Christian Leadership Conference is a Civil Rights organization started in 1957. MLK was the 1 st president. It was started to help groups come together that were protesting racism and to make their efforts stronger together.

Coretta Scott King-Civil Rights Leader and wife of MLK. She founded the MLK Center for Nonviolent Change and was able to get MLK's birthday recognized as a national holiday.

Voting Rights Act of 1965-President Lyndon B. Johnson signed the law that removed obstacles that stopped African Americans from being able to vote.

Square- Shape with 4 sides & 4 angles.
Circle- Shape that is round with no sides.
Hexagon-Shape 6 sides & 6 angles.
Oval- Round & elongated shape.
Parellelogram- Shape with 4 sides where opposite sides are parallel.